How to GROW a GARDEN

MAGIC CAT PUBLISHING

To Horatio and Sacha, my two wonderful nephews, who helped me turn a book into an adventure —F.T.

For my niece Ava, who I hope will enjoying pointing at everything —C.A.

MAGIC CAT PUBLISHING

The illustrations were created using gouache
Set in Set in Catalina Clemente, Wild Soul, and Fanciful Persons
Library of Congress Control Number is 2024938813
ISBN 978-1-917044-23-3

Text copyright © 2025 Frances Tophill
Illustrations copyright © 2025 Charlotte Ager
Book design by Nicola Price
Edited by Jenny Broom

First published in North America in 2024 by Magic Cat Publishing, an imprint of Lucky Cat Publishing Ltd,
Unit 2, Empress Works, 24 Grove Passage, London E2 9FQ, UK

Printed and bound in Guangdong, China
10 9 8 7 6 5 4 3 2 1

Distributed by ABRAMS
195 Broadway, New York, NY 10007, USA

MIX
Paper | Supporting
responsible forestry
FSC® C104723
www.fsc.org

INTRODUCTION

The natural world is a magnificent, magical place.

We often look without really seeing the incredible sights that greet our eyes. If aliens landed on this planet they would think they had found the most beautiful place in the universe. And yet it's so easy to miss what surrounds us.

Each page of this book has a different type of garden to explore, from places filled with flowers, to deep, dark woodlands, secretive hedgerows, vegetable patches, silvery streams, and even hot, humid greenhouses.

As you move through each garden, discover which plants are perfectly adapted to grow and survive in the different conditions you find there—from hot to cold, and wet to dry, there really is a plant for every place.

Turn the pages and you will see that within these gardens is a whole other world, where species live and work together—and suddenly the magic of the world becomes more and more clear. At the end of each chapter you will find activities to help you grow, harvest, and care for some of these plants in your own garden.

So, let's begin our mysterious journey of unpacking what you see and making sense of nature.

Because the more you understand it, the more magical it is.

Trust me.

This is a journey through
many kinds of gardens, all
filled with plants perfectly
suited to each place.

Creatures scuttle through the
undergrowth, buzz through the air,
and burrow through the soil
beneath our toes.

Follow us as we
care for the plants and
help protect them
for the future!

CONTENTS

FLOWERS & HERBS

Here is a place filled with shrubs and flower beds.
These spaces bring together beautiful colors,
scents, and sounds—all for you to enjoy!

Most of the flowers in this section are "hardy ornamentals." As a rule, if plants are growing outside in the decorative areas of the garden, rather than the wild areas, then they will be hardy ornamentals.

"Hardy" means that a plant can withstand very cold temperatures, while "ornamental" means that they are attractive to look at. (In our opinion, this is a bit silly to say, as many plants, like vegetables, are just as beautiful.)

Let's go and discover
some together!

FLOWER GARDEN
This is a world filled with flowers in the summer . . .

But by winter, they will all be gone. The flowers come in all kinds of colors and sizes. Some are tall, others are tiny and hug the ground. They grow in flower beds, which are sometimes called "herbaceous borders."

HOLLYHOCKS

SISYRINCHIUM

Herbaceous plants are *green* and *soft* and die each year when the weather turns cold, to regrow in spring.

Irises have a little flap that knocks *pollen* off a bee's back as it climbs into the flower, fertilizing it. The bee climbs back out, covered in the plant's own pollen, and carries it to the next flower.

It's easy for **weeds** to hide and grow here! But we don't mind them too much—everything is welcome in our garden.

In winter, some of the stems stay upright and are covered in *seeds* the birds can eat.

CROCOSMIA

DELPHINIUM

Leave all these plants here through the winter to help caterpillars, beetles, worms, flies, spiders, and lizards, who live in the soil and *dead plant material* on the floor.

CONEFLOWER

Some of the flowers here, like delphiniums and hollyhocks, are *big* and *tall* so that the bees can see them from a long way off.

IRIS

HERB GARDEN

In our Mediterranean herb garden, water is scarce.

Plants here are baked by sunlight and the soil is full of
rocks, so even if rain does fall, the water quickly soaks away.
In this bright, light landscape, you can see for miles, so plants
produce colorful flowers that the bees can see from far off.

EUCALYPTUS

Many of the plants here have
medicinal properties.

Lavender
makes us feel
calm.

Rosemary
improves our
memory.

HYSSOP

LAVENDER

Hyssop helps fight off
coughs and colds.

Some *insects* even use
these plants to make
themselves feel better!

THYME

ROSEMARY

TEA TREE

These plants often
grow furry or small *waxy*
leaves that help them hold
on to the small amount of
moisture that's here.

Many of these plants have developed strong-smelling leaves that are delicious to us, but put *animals* off eating them.

DITTANY

OLIVE TREE

PINE

The warm air is filled with the thick *scent* of herbs and the sound of buzzing insects.

APPLE MINT

Biomes are regions with similar climates that support similar plants and animals. The Mediterranean biome includes the Mediterranean Basin, California, central Chile, southern Australia, and parts of South Africa.

WHITE HOREHOUND

MULLEIN

ROCK GARDEN

Here, plants cling to the edges of rocks and clamber over stones.

The plants have specially adapted suckers and pads to climb up vertical rocks, rubble and boulders, but their roots have little space while the light is bright and strong, so nothing grows too tall.

In the nooks and crannies between the rocks, all kinds of *creatures* hide away from predators.

MOUNTAIN PINE

HYDRANGEA

SPEEDWELL

PASQUE FLOWER

CLIMBING HYDRANGEA

LITHODORA

LILACBUSH

BALKAN ANEMONE

VIRGINIA CREEPER

ROSEMARY

IVY

BLUE STAR JUNIPER

DELOSPERMA

SEA THRIFT

DIANTHUS

These plants have small but *strong root systems* that cling to tiny soil patches, but stay strong in high winds.

FLEABANE

THYME

Plants grow *short* and *stocky* here, so the wind doesn't uproot them from the shallow soil.

SEA LAVENDER

PHLOX

⚘ SPRING ⚘

Plant for Pollinators: Sow a Sunflower Seed

Fill a pot with compost, wet it, then make a hole in the center with your finger.
Put a sunflower seed into the hole, cover it over with compost, and firm it down with your fingers.

Keep your pot warm and slightly damp until the first shoots poke through the compost.

Once the weather really warms up, slowly get your plant used to being outside by putting it out during the day for one week and bringing it in at night. Then, plant it in the garden and wait for the bees to buzz by!

❋ SUMMER ❋

Healing Herbs: Grow Mint

Fill a little pot with compost and water it so it's damp. Then, make a hole in the compost.

Cut a sprig of healthy growth off some mint. Snip the bottom of your stem just below a set of leaves. Then, remove all the leaves and any flower buds, leaving only the top set of leaves. Put this stem into the hole in the compost and firm all the compost around it so it's gently touching the stem.

Keep it on the windowsill, and water it when it dries out. In a couple of months, roots will appear at the bottom of the pot.

You can pick some mint leaves and pour hot water over them to make a healthy mint tea.

❧ AUTUMN ❧

Plant Daffodils for the Spring

Go to the garden centre and buy some daffodil bulbs. They look brown and papery with a pointy top and a rooty, flat bottom.

Dig a hole that's three times the length of the bulb. Place the bulb into the hole with the rooty end down. Bury it in the ground and smooth over all the soil so you can't even see where it is. It'll be a lovely surprise when it grows and flowers in February or March!

If you don't have a garden, you can plant bulbs into pots in exactly the same way, just make sure you keep them outside as they don't like to be stuck indoors.

❧ WINTER ❧

Welcome the Wildlife

Don't cut everything back and make your garden too neat. Winter is a perfect excuse to be messy!

Brown stalks, mushy stems, and leaves on the ground provide all kinds of places for small animals and creepy crawlies to hide—and all kinds of foods for birds and little creatures to eat when it's cold.

Wrap up warm and try sitting very still and see if you can spot any creatures.

TREES

Trees are some of the biggest things to have ever lived on Earth—bigger even than dinosaurs!

Trees can be ancient, too. The Fortingall Yew in Scotland is one of the oldest living things in the world. Some experts think it could be 5,000 years old! Just think of what it has lived through . . . centuries passing, battles raging, villages and towns springing up across the countryside and crumbling back to the ground again.

It is quite mystifying.

ANCIENT WOODLAND

In the woods, you can feel the wilderness start to encroach.

These peaceful places are teeming with life: dormice scurry below, while buzzards survey the land from above. In spring, before the leaves come out and the warmth and light of the sun can still reach the ground, the ancient woodland floor is a carpet of wildflowers.

HAZEL

Hazels have male flowers called *catkins* and female flowers that look like little red tassels.

Trees that lose their *leaves* in autumn are called deciduous or broadleaf. These trees flower and fruit.

BLUEBELL

WOOD ANEMONE

Conifers have **needles** or scales and most species stay green all year.

PINE

LIME

Conifers produce **cones** instead of flowers, some with pollen and others with seeds or nuts. You may have eaten pine nuts in food like pesto!

Some broadleaf trees, like **holly**, keep their leaves year-round.

BURNING BUSH

HOLLY

MAPLE

DOUGLAS FIR

Maples, ginkgo, and Persian ironwood are bright in *autumn*.

GINKGO

RHODODENDR

GRAND SPECIMEN TREES

These trees stand proud and tall.

For centuries, people have traveled the world and brought back specimen trees to plant in an arboretum, like this. The word "specimen" comes from the Latin meaning "to look at."

Grand old conifers like Douglas firs and giant sequoias come from **North America.**

The monkey puzzle, with its shiny, vicious spikes, comes from the mountains of *Chile.*

MONKEY PUZZLE

GIANT SEQUOIA

Rhododendrons, magnolias, and camellias come from *Asia.*

The tallest, oldest, and widest trees are called *champions.*

Arbor means "tree" in Latin, and *arboretum* means "a place with "trees."

CAMELLIA

19

SOIL

You may think the ground isn't as alive as the trees.

But think again. Down here is a dark and deep and secret world, home to tiny, busy creatures and organisms that we are only just beginning to understand.

Soil is made up of sand, silt, clay, and dead matter that slowly decays into compost. It is filled with *nutrients* that plants need to grow.

Fungi may look small on the surface, but they are actually the biggest organisms on earth. Deep below the soil, they have root systems called mycelium that grow for miles.

The tiny *mycelium* threads attach to roots, providing a network for trees to share nutrients, water, and even news of danger.

MYCELIUM

FUNGI

The soil is teeming with invisible *microscopic* life, like bacteria and single-celled protozoa.

PROTOZOA

☘ SPRING ☘

Make a Log Pile

After the storms of winter, gather fallen branches, small sticks, and little twigs to make insect habitats.

Simply pile your gathered wood on the ground, somewhere protected and out of the way of people, dogs, and foxes, so that all kinds of creatures can make this their home for the year—or even longer!

If you have a garden with trees you could do this at home, but you could also try it in a park or woodland near you, too. Just make sure it isn't too windy!

❀ SUMMER ❀

Look at Leaves

Observe and make drawings of the leaves from different species of tree.

Is the leaf big or small?

Is it a single leaf, or do multiple leaflets make up a bigger leaf?

Is it shiny or buff or rough?

What color is it?

How quickly does it fall to the ground when you drop it?

Can you see light through it when you hold it to the sky?

❧ AUTUMN ❧

Grow a Tree from a Cutting

Fill a pot with soil or compost. Get an adult to help you cut a piece of long, straight growth from an elder, hazel, or willow tree.

Cut the stem into pieces, making sure there is a bud or two at the top and bottom of each piece.

Push each stem into the pot as deep as you can. Try to make sure two buds are under the soil and one sticks out above the soil.

Keep the pot outside, and water it every now and then. Leave it for a year, and next winter you should find it has made roots of its own, ready to plant in the ground.

❧ WINTER ❧

Plant a Tree for the Future

In the winter, you can buy trees with no pots or soil, just bare roots. Trees can stay like this, above the soil, for quite a while, as long as they are watered. A lot of environmental programs even give free trees to schools and communities.

Choose a tree that's native to your area so that it has the most benefits to the wildlife there. Dig a hole and plant your tree, making sure the roots are covered and the soil is firmed up. Water it well during its first year, especially when it's hot.

You can come back all through your life and see how big it has grown. Some trees will live for centuries!

HEDGES & EDGES

Many people walk past hedges, thinking they aren't worth bothering to look at. But those people would be wrong.

Hedges are places for all sorts of furtive creatures to live under cover and stay hidden away.

Many of our gardens and parks have hedges and edges all around them. And these places can be found out in the world, too: even roadsides and railway lines can act as huge living corridors where creatures can run around, safe from people and predators.

These are really important habitats that we often forget to notice.

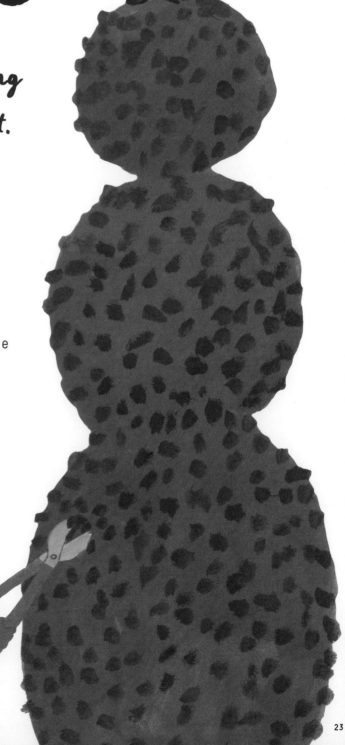

NATIVE HEDGES

Hedgerows can be scrappy, messy places.
People often plant them to keep us out of areas they don't want us to go. The chances are that you might not notice them or pay much attention to them. But native hedgerows are absolutely teeming with life!

In spring, some native hedge species, like blackthorn, produce clusters of flowers that *smell* lovely.

HAWTHORN

BLACKTHORN

WILD CHERVIL

Stop by a hedge and listen, especially at dawn, or when it's getting dark. You will hear all kinds of *scurrying* sounds made by birds, mice, lizards, spiders, woodlice, caterpillars, and butterflies.

These hedges are not cut too neatly and are full of living and dead wood, which means you'll find all kinds of *fungus* here, too.

Species like *hawthorn* produce berries in winter, and their spikes keep out the predators, so small birds and mice love these places.

Native hedgerow plants have grown here since the last Ice Age (about 10,000 years ago), so the creatures know the plants well and which bits they can eat.

Yews can be clipped and clipped and clipped into neat shapes by gardeners on tall ladders. You can even cut a window or a door into a hedge, to see or walk through.

CLIPPED HEDGES

Hedges can be majestic beings.

Every time these shrub and tree species are cut, they branch more and more—until the branches are so dense and tangled that you can't even see through. That's the point of hedges. To keep a place private.

BOXWOOD

Listen. What do you hear?
Rustling maybe, or birds
singing their songs. All kinds of
birds nest in clipped hedges.

Some hedges are planted
in *two rows.* Squeeze
yourself in and run between
the two . . . It's a little bit
naughty, but lots of fun!

YEW

The hedge roots take
all the water while
the leaves take all
the light, so not much
grows underneath . . .
But small *creatures*
like to dig here!

WEEDS
What is a weed?

This is a difficult question to answer. Weeds are just plants, but these species often grow quickly and spread their roots far and wide. As a result, they are the plants that people love to hate! Even though some people think weeds are bad, they are essential to wildlife and often useful to us, too.

Nettles can sting if you touch them. But some butterfly species lay their eggs here, and their caterpillars eat the leaves.

NETTLE

DANDELION

Bindweed has white roots that spread a long way beneath the soil. Just one of these roots can regrow a whole plant. That's why most people think of it as a weed.

I don't know why some gardeners hate *dandelions.* You can eat every part, from the roots to the buds, and they have all kinds of health benefits.

The convolvulus hawk-moth depends on *bindweed* flowers to survive.

My guinea pig loves dandelions!

BINDWEED

FEVERFEW

YARROW

❀ SPRING ❀

Pick Stinging Nettles for Soup

This is a challenging one! Try it in March or April, when the nettles are very young and they can't be confused with anything else that might hurt you.

Pop on a pair of gloves and pick the newly grown nettle leaves. At home, add them to potato soup for a delicious and nutritious feast!

Remember, even if you do get stung, the stings are good for you—nettles are used to treat all sorts of illnesses. So, it might hurt, but it won't do you harm.

Avoid nettles from roads (which are covered in exhaust fumes) or paths (which are probably covered in dog pee)!

❀ SUMMER ❀

Check for Biodiversity

Biodiversity simply refers to how diverse the biology of a place is—in other words, how many different things live there. So, count how many different species you can find living and growing in your local park or garden. Don't forget to include all the hedges, trees, and weeds—even the ones in the grass.

The more plant species there are, the better that is for biodiversity, so in theory there will be far more insects, mammals, birds, reptiles, and even fungi living there.

AUTUMN

Sow a Native Plant

Sow a seed of a native tree or hedge plants. Most of these species prefer their seeds to be sown in autumn, then left outside in the cold to germinate in spring.

Gather nuts or fruits from the hedgerows, take out the seeds in the center (this might get a bit sticky!), and pot them up into compost.

Leave them outside all winter, somewhere safe from rats and squirrels. Make sure they don't dry out, and keep your fingers crossed! Hopefully, in late spring—or even next spring, because sometimes it takes two cold winters to break the though seed coating— brand new little trees will shoot up.

WINTER

Welcome the Wildlife

Winter is a tough time to be a little animal. So, it's really important at this time of year to provide some food and even warm shelter for wildlife.

Apples cut in half will feed all kinds of birds. Hang them high up, away from rats.

Nuts, seeds, and fat balls help keep birds nice and plump through the winter.

Boxes hung up high for birds, or piles of leaves on the ground for frogs, provide safety and warmth.

GRASS

Crickets rub their legs in the spacious and green grass, making songs that creak in our ears.

Where the grass is short, we can take off our shoes and feel the soft blades between our toes. Where it is long, we can lie down, hidden to everyone around, while the wind whips through the tall, swaying stems.

We lie on our backs and look up at the clouds, but other creatures are more cautious. They can be spotted by buzzards or hawks by day, and owls by night.

Only the brave and the strong, like foxes and badgers, come here without fear.

WILDFLOWER MEADOW

Here, the grass is long and the wildflowers are allowed to grow, making it a haven for wildlife.

Butterflies and lizards bask in the sunshine. Where the grass is left completely unclipped, you'll hear crickets chirruping all through the late summer and see birds foraging for seeds all through the winter!

Annual *wildflowers* germinate from a seed, grow, flower, produce new seeds, and then die, all in a single season.

COMMON VETCH

Some years are cold and wet, while other years are hot and dry . . . Different *conditions* favor different plants, so the meadow never looks the same!

MUSK MALLOW

RAGGED ROBIN

Be careful of **spiky plants** on your bare feet!

YELLOW HORNPOPPY

Many people think of wildflowers as **weeds**, but they are pretty, and their roots don't spread through the ground and take over.

KNAPWEED

CORNFLOWER

The grass is cut once or twice a year, and is left uncleared for a while so that the **seeds** can land on the floor, ready for next year.

Yellow hornpoppies, oxeye daisies, cornflowers, *field scabious*, vetch, knapweed, campion, ragged robin, and orchids all grow here.

OXEYE DAISY

FIELD SCABIOUS

WEEPING
WILLOW

There are nearly 12,000
grass species around the world!
One of the most common types
of lawn grass in the U.S. is
Kentucky bluegrass,
which grows quickly and is
resistant to cold.

Fescues and *bentgrass*
lie low, their thin blades
spreading neatly.

STRIPED LAWN

Dark green, pale green, dark green, pale green . . .

From the lawn, the views stretch far and wide. Not many plants can cope with being walked on, but grass can, so it's perfect for us to play and run on, enjoying the open space and feeling of freedom. Lawns are so much better than plastic turf because the grass can cope with rain, and allows excess water to slowly drain away.

In some gardens, a lawn of *chamomile* is planted, which releases soft fragrance from the leaves as we walk on it.

CHAMOMILE

Seagulls do a rain dance to bring up worms.

RYEGRASS

❧ SPRING ❧

Plant a Meadow

You can get buy many kinds of wildflower seeds. Buy some peat-free seed compost, and a module tray with at least twelve mini pots. Or, save old toilet rolls and fill them with compost instead.

Wet the compost, then drop a seed or two into each module. Scatter compost over the seeds, pat it down, then sprinkle with water. Keep the seeds damp until you see them sprouting.

Once they're big enough, plant them into the lawn. Don't break them up—just plant the whole module or toilet roll into each hole.

Soon they will grow with the grass into a meadow!

❀ SUMMER ❀

No Mow May

No Mow May encourages gardeners not to mow their lawns until the end of May, giving animals a safe place to hide and forage.

The problem is that when we mow again in June, small animals can get injured by our lawn cutting tools. So, before you mow, get a stick and slowly walk through the long grass, bashing as you go and making as much noise as possible to scare off any animals before the lawn mower or strimmer gets near them.

Another good thing to do is leave a little patch of safe space that is never mowed.

🍂 AUTUMN 🍂

Collect Seeds for Spring

Seeds can be gathered now for wildflowers next spring. Wildflowers that naturally grow in your area are the most useful to the creatures that live there.

Wait for a sunny day, and when the dew has dried, go into a local meadow to collect seed heads. (Go with an adult who will be able to tell flowers from weeds!) Scatter the seeds under hedges and around other places you'd like them to grow.

You can also leave the seeds to really dry out on the windowsill first, then store them in a dark, cool, dry place until next spring, when you start your wildflower sowing again.

❄ WINTER ❄

Write to Your Local Council Members

Many local councils are getting better at grassland management: they leave more wildflowers and long grass to grow on road verges than ever before.

But there is still more work to do!

Perhaps you'd like your council to plant more trees in your local park, or set aside more land for growing fruit and vegetables. (If you get a group together to do this then the council have to give you land—it's the law!)

Whatever you think, write to them and tell them. It will remind the council that we all care about the world we live in. And that will encourage them to protect it even more.

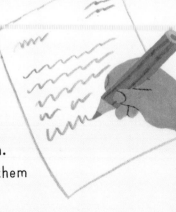

FRUIT & VEGETABLES

We think that fruits and vegetables can be just as pretty as flowers . . . and better, too, because you can eat them!

Since olden times, parts of the garden like this have supplied us with fresh vegetables, fruit for eating and juicing, and also with lovely flowers to cut and take inside.

Vegetables are some of the hardest things to grow and it takes a lot of time to keep everything watered and healthy.

But nothing beats eating your own freshly-grown food!

In spring, the trees are full of blossoms, which pollinating insects love. In autumn, wasps and hornets feast on the *fruit* that have dropped to the ground.

ORCHARD

An orchard is a space with six or more fruit trees.

Apricots, peaches, and almonds ripen in the warmest and sunniest spots, while elsewhere apples, pears, plums, cherries, and even strange, old-fashioned fruits like quinces and medlars grow. You might also find a nuttery where all sorts of nuts are grown, like walnuts, hazelnuts, cashews, almonds, and pecans.

Many kinds of *birds* love to come and eat the fruits. (You can imagine how the gardeners feel about that!)

APPLE TREE

APRICOT TREE

PLUM TREE

It's warm in the sun, but never too hot under the *shade* of the canopy.

Some people call medlars a delicacy, but they look like a dog's bottom and you eat them when they go a bit *rotten*!

MEDLAR TREE

The *hothouse* is sunk into the ground for extra heat, making it perfect for growing exotic fruits.

STRAWBERRY

ORANGE

LEMON

BLUEBERRY

REDCURRANT

Scrumptious soft *fruits* like raspberries, strawberries, blackcurrants, gooseberries, redcurrants, blackberries, grapes, and blueberries grow here, too.

CARROT

KALE

SCALLION

SWEET PEA

VEGETABLE GARDEN

This is the crown jewel of the whole garden.

My mouth waters just thinking about all these amazing things to eat. Flower beds all around the edge bring in the pollinating insects that are needed to grow some fruits and vegetables, while companion plants like borage, marigolds, and phacelia bring even more color while helping the crops to flourish.

RASPBERRY

The sun-baked walls of the **greenhouse** keep *in* the heat and keep *out* the wind, as well as rabbits, deer, and other hungry animals!

TOMATO

BUG HOTEL

Edibles like cucumbers, tomatoes, chilies, peppers, eggplants, and sweet potatoes grow in the *greenhouse*.

Sprouts, kale, leeks, spinach, chard, salad, arugula, mustard, peas, butter beans, zucchini, carrots, parsnips, turnips, pumpkins, and all sorts of other *vegetables* here do best outside.

PEA

GARDEN SHED

This is where gardeners sow seeds and take cuttings.

It is also a place to store and dump things, and in these forgotten corners there are all kinds of tiny creatures, like millipedes, woodlice, wasps, and spiders. Some people are afraid of creepy-crawlies, but these fascinating creatures are essential to our ecosystem. They eat the tiny pests, like aphids, that feed on our plants, and they munch on garden waste and help to break it down.

The **compost heap** is where plant materials decompose. Once everything breaks down it will feed the soil with its amazing goodness.

LEAF MOLD

COMPOST

The fallen leaves of autumn are piled up in the *leaf bays* until they turn to leaf mold, another kind of compost.

Heat is produced as the plants break down, and mice and bumblebees nest in these *warm places*.

That heat is caused by the activity of millions of *bacteria, fungi,* and other tiny creatures working their way through all of that material.

❧ SPRING ❧

Sow Your Own Dinner

This is the perfect time for growing vegetables from seed, like carrots, peas, pumpkins, and kale!

Put the seed compost in a planting tray. Dampen it, scatter on the seeds, then cover with a thin layer of compost roughly three times the depth of the seeds.

Put the tray by a window or somewhere warm.

Keep the seeds nicely damp.

As soon as you see leaves growing, reduce watering so the seedlings don't get fungus rotting their stems.

Sow carrot, parsnip, or beetroot seeds straight into the pot they are going to grow in: they don't like to be moved!

❧ SUMMER ❧

Spread the Joy of Plants

Plant out your crops from May onwards. Some quick crops, like peas, may already be quite big. Make sure you allow plenty of space around each plant.

Lots of fruit and vegetables will soon be ready to pick and eat, fresh from the vine! Beans, peas, tomatoes, peppers, lettuce, and summer fruits, too, like strawberries, are the taste of summer!

If you have extra food, set up a "help yourself" fruit and vegetable stand outside your house. You could also donate leftovers to a food bank.

❧ AUTUMN ❧

Compost Your World

Harvest vegetables like carrots, parsnips, and kale in the autumn. If you've grown pumpkins, then you can carve them for Halloween!

When you have taken all that you like, this is the perfect time to make some lovely and rich compost.

Cut all the stems into sections of about 8 inches long and chop up the leaves. Try not to put too many weeds with roots on the compost.

Do include some woody stems, like the gnarled ones from the pumpkins.

Make a pile and fork it over every now and then until it's lovely and soft.

❧ WINTER ❧

Feed Your Soil

Sprinkle a layer of manure onto the ground, along with either last year's homemade compost, or store-bought peat-free compost. This is called mulch.

Mulch feeds the soil, it keeps the water in, and it stops the weeds in the soil from germinating.

That's all you have to do! You don't even need to dig mulch into the soil, because when your soil is healthy, the worms and minibeasts will slowly chew through it, then go down into the depths again, so the mulch slowly moves down into the lower levels.

WATER

Water is essential to wildlife: some species come to bathe and drink, while others live in it permanently!

We're not just talking about glistening ponds and trickling streams, but also wetlands and bogs, where the ground squelches beneath our feet. In these watery habitats you'll find frogs, newts, fish, and aquatic insects. So much life!

Ponds and wetlands channel and store rainwater, which keeps animals and plants alive during long, dry periods. Some of these places might seem soggy and muddy at times, but water is so important to all living things . . . *including us!*

BOG GARDEN

Even if you can't see the water, the ground in the bog garden is moist all of the time.

The earth feels soft and damp. When the sun shines, the huge leaves in different shades of green and the iridescent flowers standing as tall as your head can make you feel like you are surrounded by a forest of jewels.

Some plants, like meadowsweet, *smell beautiful.*

GUNNERA

LIGULARIA

MEADOWSWEET

HORSETAIL

RODGERSIA

There is *no air* in the bog, only water in the earth. Some bog plants, like horsetail, grow hollow, air-filled stems to survive. Others grow roots way above the soil and breathe through those.

CANDELABRA PRIMROSE

Some bog plants have **evolved** to grow pink and yellow flowers, which attract a variety of insects in the dark dampness.

Plants here never have to worry about losing too much *moisture* through their leaves, so gunnera, umbrella plants, and even rhubarb grow leaves as big as you can imagine.

Other plants, like *stinky* skunk cabbage, smell horrible!

SKUNK CABBAGE

ROYAL FERN

STREAM AND POND

The stream water flows quickly.

The sun shines on the ripples and rapids, and the stones are smoothed by years of hurrying water. You can hear the stream as it rushes through the little valley toward the large pond, where it finds stillness and rest among the reeds.

Frogs, toads, newts, brown eels, water beetles, and water scorpions can all be found in the pond if you dare to dip your *net* in and inspect the mud it brings up. Be gentle, and put these aquatic creatures back in the water as soon as you can!

WATER LILY

Pond snails, water louse, leeches, and other grubs live in the sludge at the bottom of the pond.

Birds come for a bath, splashing in the shallows and throwing water all around.

The pond is surrounded by **reeds, bulrushes,** and **bog plants.**

BULRUSH

WEEPING WILLOW

Swallows swoop in the swift flow to scoop up a drink, while little fish dart upstream.

Dragonfly wings glisten in the sunshine as they dart about, eventually settling on a still reed to lay their eggs in the water.

Water boatmen lunge their long legs to propel themselves along the surface, leaving long streaks of ripples behind them.

TROPICAL POND

The largest greenhouse is warm and moist, and in the middle is a huge pool of water.

There is real magic here. The plants are huge and impressive, and it's easy to get distracted by them. But, if you sit quietly, waiting and watching, you will see that there is so much more than meets the eye...

WATER HYACINTH

Dwarfing everything is the *Victoria lily*. Its leaves are like round rafts, are almost 10 feet wide, and it produces huge, stunning flowers around 15.5 inches wide.

The lily's *lotus* flowers grow to the size of a dinner plate in bright, zinging colors.

LOTUS

Victoria lily's scientific name—*Victoria amazonica*—tells you it comes from the *Amazon* Rainforest.

VICTORIA LILY

You could keep *tropical fish* or even piranhas here! But the gardeners in their waders cutting back the water hyacinth might not like that!

Papyrus grows on the edges of the pond, tall and elegant, with an umbrella of leaves at the tip.

The ancient Egyptians used papyrus to make *paper*.

PAPYRUS

VICTORIA LILY

❀ SPRING ❀

Watch the Water Wildlife

Go to a pond, lake, or stream with an adult and closely observe the water. What animals use it? How often do they visit?

Make an underwater viewer to see what's happening beneath the surface of the water. Take a plastic bottle and, with an adult's help, cut off the top and bottom. (Careful of any sharp edges.) Stretch some clear plastic over one end, and hold it in place with a rubber band and duct tape.

Lower the plastic-covered end into the water, look into the tube from the top and watch the wildlife below, being very careful not to fall in!

❀ SUMMER ❀

Go Pond Dipping

Be very careful while doing this activity: you don't want to hurt any of the creatures living in your pond.

With an adult's help, collect some pond water in a tray or bucket. Next, use a fine net to scoop some silt from the bottom of the pond and place it in the container.

Soon, the aquatic creatures will begin to emerge from the silt: maybe dragonfly nymphs, tadpoles, or water fleas! Count how many different species you find before gently releasing them back into the pond.

🍂 AUTUMN 🍂

Prepare Your Pond for Winter

Ask an adult to help you pick out any fallen leaves from the pond to keep it clean.

Float a little plastic ball in the water so that if the surface freezes over, the creatures down there can still breathe.

If you're in a very cold place and are worried your pond might freeze completely, you could cover it with horticultural fleece or a cloche, or even a mini greenhouse to stop it freezing right to the bottom!

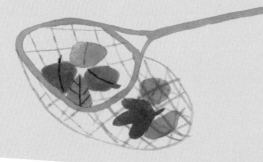

🌿 WINTER 🌿

Build a New Pond!

Dig a hole and stick an old washing-up bowl into the ground. Choose somewhere that gets morning sun but isn't in the full sunshine all day—you could even use a shrub in a pot to create shade.

Fill the bowl with water and construct a slope of rocks, so that if an animal falls in, it can climb back out again.

Place two pond plants into the water—an oxygenator, and a reed or shallow aquatic plant. (Ask for advice at a garden center.)

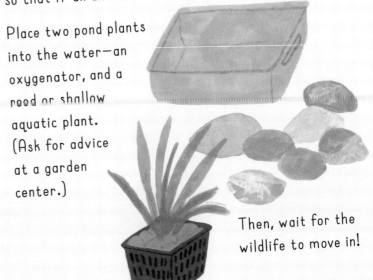

Then, wait for the wildlife to move in!

EXOTIC PLANTS

Welcome to a world of weird and wonderful plants.

There are exotic plants in here, of all shapes and sizes, that have come from other parts of the world where the climate can be very different to ours at home. To help them grow, we must protect them indoors, under glass, out of the cold, wet, and wind.

The scented flowers attract different kinds of pollinators. Moths, who fly at night, love sweet, reflective white flowers, while all kinds of huge and amazing butterflies live alongside the tropical plants.

Everything here loves the balmy warmth.

ARID GARDEN

These plants are from the driest places on Earth.

Many of these plants look mean and scary. In the deserts, mountains, and tundras where they grow, there is very little for animals to eat or drink, so the plants come up with all kinds of ways to avoid being munched and hold onto moisture!

The light is clear and bright, so plants grow huge flowers that shoo up above the rest of th landscape, to be seen b *pollinators* for miles around.

BARREL CACTUS

AGAVE

BARBARY FIG

Cacti are covered from tip to toe in vicious *spikes*. This stops animals like goats, sheep, rabbits, and camels from eating them.

PONYTAIL PALM

Here, euphorbia grows as a **candelabra tree**—tall, greeny-gray, and elephantine. It looks like a tree, but really it's a succulent with white, sticky sap that burns your skin if you touch it.

YUCCA

CANDELABRA TREE

PRICKLY PEAR

SAGUARO

Many plants here, like aloes, have fleshy, moist centers. This adaptation is called *succulence*.

The plants here don't need heat, but hate **wet** soil.

MAMMILLARIA

ALOE VERA

55

Cycads are palm-like plants that first grew *280 million years ago*—way before dinosaurs!

TROPICAL GARDEN

The air is thick with moisture . . .

It's warm, too. These plants are from rainforests. Mist, dew and rain collect and run down in huge droplets to the tips of the foliage, before tumbling and sploshing onto the floor. Climbers sprawl up the trunks of the big tropical palms, which cast shadows with their huge leaves.

VENUS FLYTRAP

BIRD OF PARADISE

With lots of warmth, moisture and nutrients, plants can make their flowers as big and *bright* as they like for insects to spot.

HIBISCUS

The **corpse flower** has the tallest bloom of any plant, while the *giant padma* produces the single largest individual flower in the world!

Some of our favorite *foods* grow here: chocolate from cacao trees, banana, mango, and papaya.

CYCAD

The pollinators here are different: *flies.* So sometimes, instead of smelling sweet, their scent is like rotting flesh.

CACAO TREE

CORPSE FLOWER

GIANT PADMA

PITCHER PLANT

Carnivorous plants, like Venus flytraps and pitcher plants, trap and eat bugs, and sometimes small mammals and birds!

In rainforests, sunlight is scarce, so plants have grown larger and larger leaves to *catch any drop of light* that makes it past the tree canopy to the ground.

FERNERY

Step into a dark, damp world.

The fernery is tucked away, deep in the woods. This is a place of gorgeous greenery and earthy smells. The ferns here love moisture and shade, so the greenhouse is sunk into the ground, and mosses climb the damp stone walls.

Some ferns can be huge, like *tree ferns* from Australasia. Others are tiny, barely visible ferns that ramble along the ground or up tree trunks.

Ferns evolved long before flowers. They don't need insects to pollinate them and they don't produce seeds. Instead, they release tiny *spores* which spread on the wind.

HART'S TONGUE FERN

TREE FERN

Amazing species like *mosses* and *liverworts* form on the surfaces of stone and soil.

SILVER FERN

Lichens are a complex life form that grow when green algae and fungus join together. Lichens can be crusty, leaf-like, or bushy, but they never have roots or stems!

MAIDENHAIR FERN

Ferns have the most *beautiful fronds*. They are mostly green, though not entirely, and often let a little light through so the fronds beneath them don't starve.

TASSEL FERN

ALPINE GARDEN

Come inside the alpine house.

Gravelly beds hold pots full of little flowers and funny little fuzzy mats of plants! Tiny leaves, furry edges, and bright, delicate little flowers . . . that's what the alpine house is full of.

With tiny roots that cannot hold much water, these plants hug the floor and stay *low*, to protect themselves from cold and drying winds.

Alpine plants enjoy dry, bright, cold conditions. That's because they have evolved to grow high up on *mountains* in biting wind and snow.

BELLFLOWER

STONECROP

Plants lose moisture through their leaves. In the steamy tropical garden the leaves were huge, but here they are *tiny*, with hairs that catch moisture, and waxy skins that protect against cold and drought.

STORK'S BILL

CREEPING THYME

HOUSELEEK

For months,
these plants lie
under *snow*, waiting.
Then they must flower
quickly, sending up little
bright flowers during short
bursts of sunshine, for
pollinators to spot.

DIANTHUS

PASQUE FLOWER

❧ SPRING ❧

Sow Tomato Seeds

Did you know that tomatoes originally came from South America, and were first grown in greenhouses as an ornamental plant?

Today, you can buy a packet of tomato seeds quite cheaply and grow them on your windowsill at home. First, choose a bush variety, which is easier to grow.

Put some compost into a tray and pat it down. Scatter the seeds on the surface of the compost, then sprinkle a little more compost over the top. Place the tray into a shallow container of water, until the surface of the compost feels damp, then remove the tray again.

Keep the seeds moist and warm in a greenhouse, or by a windowsill, until the second set of leaves has formed.

Carefully lever each plant up from the roots and put them into their own pots. Keep growing them inside.

❧ SUMMER ❧

Repot Your Tomato Plants

Every time the tomatoes look like they are getting too big for their pots, move them into a bigger pot with lovely fresh compost.

Water your tomato plants—they do not like to be too wet, but also don't like to dry out.

Once the plants are big and healthy, put them into their final growing place. Bush tomatoes will keep growing in a big pot or in the ground.

❧ AUTUMN ❧

Harvest Your Tomatoes

From late summer onward, you should start to get juicy, ripe tomatoes. Remove some of the biggest leaves so that the sun will hit the fruits and help them ripen, then you can pick and eat them when they're ready. Delicious!

If you have too many and don't know what to do with them, make them into a sauce or a soup and freeze it, so that you can enjoy fresh tomatoes all winter.

Try to save some of the seeds. Soak the flesh of the fruit until the seeds separate, then dry them thoroughly on tissue paper and store them in a cool, dry, dark place until next spring.

❧ WINTER ❧

Get Ready for Your Next Crop

Clear the old stems of your tomato plants by cutting them off at the ground and throw them on the compost heap. Then get the ground ready for next year.

If you have grown your tomatoes in a pot, you'll need to clean out the pot. Sprinkle the old compost around the garden to help feed the soil. Then, get some fresh, new compost ready and start thinking about next year's tomato seeds.

Did you like these and want to grow them again?

Or will you grow something new?

GLOSSARY

ARID: an environment that is extremely dry because there isn't much rainfall

BIODIVERSITY: how many different plants and animals live in an area

CARNIVOROUS: a plant that can trap animals like insects to eat

COMPANION PLANTS: plants that help and complement each other by reducing pests and increasing pollination

COMPOST: decayed plant material that you can add to soil to give it nutrients

CUTTINGS: little pieces of a plant that have been cut off and can be used to grow a whole new plant

DECIDUOUS: trees that lose their leaves in autumn and grow new ones in spring, also called broadleaf

FERTILIZING: the process of pollen (male reproductive cell) coming into contact with the ovule (female reproductive cell), leading to the creation of a seed

GERMINATE: when a seed starts to grow

GREENHOUSE: a building made of glass that protects plants from cold and wind

HEDGEROW: a line of shrubs and trees, often planted at the side of a road or field

HERBACEOUS: soft, leafy plants with stems that aren't woody, they flower and die in winter

MYCELIUM: the root-like structure of a fungus that's made up of tiny threads

PERENNIAL: a plant that lives for more than two years rather than dying each winter

POLLEN: a fine powder that's made by the male part of a flower, used to fertilize the female egg cell

POLLINATORS: animals that carry pollen between flowers, helping to fertilize them

PROTOZOA: tiny organisms that contain only one cell (humans have 36 trillion cells!)

ROOT: the part of a plant that usually grows underground, taking in water and nutrients

SHOOT: the first part of the plant to appear above ground, when it is just starting to grow

SPORE: a cell produced by some plants and fungi that is spread by the wind and grows into a new plant

WHICH PLANT, WHICH PLACE?

A
Agave – 54
Aloe vera – 55
Apple mint – 11
Apple tree – 38
Apricot tree – 39

B
Balkan anemone – 12
Barbary fig – 54
Barrel cactus – 54
Bellflower – 60
Bindweed – 28, 29
Bird of paradise – 56
Blue star juniper – 13
Bluebell – 16
Blueberry – 40
Boxwood – 26
Bulrush – 49
Burning bush – 17

C
Cacao tree – 57
Camellia – 19
Candelabra primrose – 46
Candelabra tree – 55
Carrot – 40
Chamomile – 35
Cherry tree – 38
Climbing hydrangea – 12
Common vetch – 37
Coneflower – 9
Cornflower – 33
Corpse flower – 57
Creeping thyme – 61
Crocosmia – 9
Cycad – 57

D
Dandelion – 28
Delosperma – 13
Delphinium – 9
Dianthus – 13, 61
Dittany – 11
Douglas fir – 18

E
Eucalyptus – 10

F
Feverfew – 29
Field scabious – 33
Fleabane – 13
Fungi – 20

G
Giant padma – 57
Giant sequoia – 19
Ginkgo – 18
Gunnera – 46

H
Hart's tongue fern – 58
Hawthorn – 24
Hazel – 16
Hibiscus – 56
Holly – 17
Hollyhocks – 8
Horsetail – 46
Houseleek – 61
Hydrangea – 12
Hyssop – 10

I
Iris – 9
Ivy – 13

K
Kale – 40
Knapweed – 33

L
Lavender – 10
Leaf mold – 43
Lemon – 40
Ligularia – 46
Lilacbush – 12
Lime – 17
Lithodora – 12
Lotus – 50

M
Maidenhair fern – 59
Mammillaria – 55
Maple – 18
Meadowsweet – 46
Medlar tree – 39
Monkey puzzle – 19
Mountain pine – 12
Mullein – 11
Musk mallow – 32
Mycelium – 20

N
Nettle – 28

O
Olive tree – 11
Orange – 40
Oxeye daisy – 33

P
Papyrus – 51
Pasque flower – 12, 61
Pea – 41
Phlox – 13
Pine – 11, 17
Pitcher plant – 57
Plum tree – 39
Ponytail palm – 55
Prickly pear – 55
Protozoa – 20

R
Ragged robin – 33
Raspberry – 41
Redcurrant – 40
Rhododendron – 18
Rodgersia – 46
Rosemary – 10, 13
Royal fern – 47

S
Saguaro – 55
Scallion – 40
Sea lavender – 13
Sea poppy – 33
Sea thrift – 13
Stonecrop – 60
Silver fern – 59
Sisyrinchium – 8
Skunk cabbage – 47
Speedwell – 12

Stork's bill – 60
Strawberry – 40

T
Tassel fern – 59
Tea tree – 10
Thyme – 10, 13
Tomato – 41
Tree fern – 59

V
Venus flytrap – 56
Victoria lily – 51
Virginia creeper – 13

W
Water hyacinth – 50
Water lily – 48
Weeping willow – 34, 49
White horehound – 11
Wild chervil – 24
Wood anemone – 16

Y
Yarrow – 29
Yew – 27
Yucca – 55